DOT'S SPOTS

Library of Congress Number: 2025904490

Clarissa Willis – Publishing Coordinator
Sharon Kizziah-Holmes – Book Design

SOLANDER
PRESS
Springdale, Arkansas

ISBN: 978-1-966675-04-4 (Paperback)
ISBN: 978-1-966675-03-7 (Hardback)
ISBN: 978-1-966675-05-1 (eBook)

Dedication

To my family and friends for their love and support. To my husband Jason, thank you for believing in me and your unwavering encouragement. You have been my beta reader, sounding board, and supportive in every way possible. Dot's Spots would not be a reality without you. To my daughter Paige, for the spark that brought this book to life. Thank you. To my sons, Jase and Chance, for reading the rough drafts and being so excited for me throughout the process.

Acknowledgments

I want to thank Clarissa Willis and Solander Press for taking a chance on me as a debut author and believing that *Dot's Spots* was worthy of publication. You have held my hand throughout the process, patiently answered my newbie questions, and provided me with an illustrator who beautifully brought my story to life. Thank you for making *Dot's Spots* a reality. I will be forever grateful.

DOT'S SPOTS

written by
Lisa Mueller

illustrated by
Kashif Qasim

Dot lived in a tiny garden with her mother.

"Why don't I have spots like yours?"

"Well, dear, you get your spots when you do good deeds for others."

Dot did not know what that meant.

Dot flew to a nearby tree to ask her friend
Molly, the spider. Before she could ask her,
she noticed that Molly was tangled in her web.
Molly was pushing and twisting but could not
break free from the sticky web.

"I knew I should have listened to my mother. She told me not to walk on the sticky parts, but I did. Now I'm stuck!"

"Don't cry, Molly. I will help you." Dot had an idea. She could chew the web apart. Dot worked hard, chewing it with the sharp edges of her tiny teeth.

Soon, Molly was free!

"Thank you! Thank you, Dot!" Molly exclaimed. "You saved me!"

Dot was overjoyed that she had been able to help her friend. "Molly, do you know what a good deed is?" Dot asked.

"Sorry, Dot. I don't know what a good deed is," replied Molly.

Dot wondered if Chester the worm would know what a good deed is.

On her way to find Chester, Dot heard someone crying. She looked down to see Chester sobbing.

Dot flew down to him and asked, "Chester, why are you crying?"

"I'm lost! I don't know how to get back home!" Chester wailed. "I was exploring, and now I don't know where I am."

"I know! I will fly up high in the sky and see if I can find your home. Then, I will come back and show you where it is."

"Thank you, Dot! Please Hurry!"

Dot stretched her tiny wings and flew as high as she could. She strained her eyes, trying to find Chester's home. Finally, she spotted a hole in the ground. Chester's mother sat beside it, looking very worried.

Dot quickly flew back to find Chester still crying. "I found your home, Chester!" It's not far from here, and I will take you there."

"There's my mother!" Chester yelled. "I'm finally home!"

Chester's mother came to greet them, and she thanked Dot for bringing Chester home.

"I'm glad I could help," Dot replied. "Chester, do you know what a good deed is?"

"No, Dot. I don't know what a good deed is. See you later."

Dot was beginning to wonder if anyone knew what a good deed was. She was sure that her caterpillar friend Josie would know.

Dot flew to the tree where Josie loved to eat leaves and was surprised to see a cocoon with a butterfly struggling to escape it. The butterfly's head was out, but she was having a hard time getting the rest of her body out of the cocoon.

"Dot! I'm so glad to see you! Can you help me?" Josie asked anxiously.

"Josie? Is that you? You're a butterfly!" Dot exclaimed.

"Yes, it's me. I can't get out of my cocoon."

She began pulling the silky cocoon with her arms. Little by little, the opening became larger, and Josie wiggled out.

"I'm free! Thank you, Dot!"

Josie stretched her wings, and she became a beautiful butterfly.

"Josie, do you know what a good deed is?"

Josie thought for a moment. "I have no idea what you are talking about."

She had one last friend to ask.

Dot flew off in search of Charlie, the ant. She spotted him struggling to carry a piece of apple.

"Hi, Charlie! What are you doing?"

"Hi, Dot. I'm trying to get this piece of apple to my home, but it's too heavy."

"Can I help?" Dot asked.

"Sure," Charlie replied.

Dot took one end of the apple, and Charlie took the other. Together, they lifted the apple and carried it to Charlie's home. The apple was very heavy, but they finally reached Charlie's anthill.

"Thank you, Dot, for helping me carry this piece of apple home."

"You're welcome, Charlie. I'm glad I could help you. I almost forgot I came to ask you if you know what a good deed is?"

"Sorry, Dot. I don't know,"

Dot flew home. She was sad. None of her friends knew what a good deed was.

"Hi, dear. You have been gone all day. What have you been doing?"

Dot noticed that her mother's eyes were wide, and she was smiling. "Why are you smiling at me, Mother?"

"I'm admiring the black spots on your back, dear."

"Spots? What spots?" Dot asked, surprised.

"These spots!" her mother answered, showing Dot her reflection in a puddle of water. Dot had four black spots, just like all the other ladybugs.

Then Dot figured it out. She had been doing good deeds when she helped others.

Dot smiled. She finally felt like a ladybug who had earned her spots.

About the Author

Lisa Mueller recently retired from a 23-year career in Special Education. She worked in many classrooms and felt rewarded for the opportunity to touch so many lives.

When not writing, you will find her reading. She knows the importance of reading to children, and her favorite quote is, "Children are made readers on the laps of their parents." Her goal is to write entertaining books that children and their caregivers enjoy.

Lisa is a SCBWI, Springfield Writers Guild, and the Oklahoma Writers Federation member. She lives in Oklahoma with her husband, daughter, and grandson.

About the Illustrator

Kashif Qasim is a professional artist living in Pakistan. He has over 20 years of experience in children's book illustration, portraits, landscape art, and sculpture. Fluent in several languages, he works internationally with authors and is best known for his free-hand digital style.

www.ingramcontent.com/pod-product-compliance
Lightning Source LLC
Chambersburg PA
CBHW041556040426

42447CB00002B/185